Body Bag

Matt Borczon

Nixes Mate Books
Allston, Massachusetts

Copyright © 2019 Matt Borczon

Book design by d'Entremont
Cover photographs from the collection of Lauren Leja

All rights reserved. This book or any portion thereof may not be reproduced or used in any manner whatsoever without the express written permission of the publisher except for the use of brief quotations in a book review or scholarly journal.

Some of these poems appeared in *Pressure Press*, *the Beatnik Cowboy*, *Stay Weird and keep writing*, and *Horror Trash Sleeze*.

Thanks and love to Dana, Hannah, Ezra Jonah and Eliza for being the reason I want to tell my story.

ISBN 978-1-949279-16-0

Nixes Mate Books
POBox 1179
Allston, MA 02134
nixesmate.pub/books

To Dr. Seward who taught my poetry writing class in Edinboro. He once read a poem I wrote and asked me why my description of Edinboro, PA was so harsh.

Body Bag

We wrapped the dead baby in a bath towel
the color of my son's eyes.

Most mornings the sound of crows in the fields
only reminds me that the child cried
for 3 days when we took her from the bed
her mother died in.

Sharp footed crows
walk across human skulls, most nights
the scratching sound keeps me awake.

During the war I dreamed of home
but it never felt real, 8 years later
home only exists in my dreams.

Dard is the Pashtu word for pain
I never learned to spell it
I still hear it in my sleep.

On the first night we were home
all the bars were filled with every soldier and marine
I served with.

When I got back from Afghanistan the weight of everything I carried would clear a room, but no one said anything except thank you for your service.

On the day I left for Afghanistan
I felt like a kid
in my fathers clothes.

Under the red white and blue
all coffins are black
on the inside.

I came home from Afghanistan
in a body bag
zipped closed from the inside.

Doctors save lives while corpsmen
sweep up bone dust
broken teeth and hair.

Cyprus was a 3 hour stop on our way
to Afghanistan, white sand and blue ocean
before the war changed everything to ash and sand.

The soldier said he didn't know
what hurt worse, stepping on the IED
or telling his wife about it the first time he called home.

All the soldiers in my therapy group agree
if we could just go back to Afghanistan
we could do it different this time.

After shift we all met for coffee officers
and enlisted, the only difference that mattered
was above or below ground.

When my son asked if I was going to die
I had no idea what to say
so I just said no.

When my father in law said war might
really change me I tried to laugh
like I thought it was funny.

Before Afghanistan I didn't know
coffins came
in children's sizes.

The first time I wiped up a big blood spill
I didn't think it would come off my hands
or out of my clothes.

I got off the night shift
on Christmas morning
and my only gift
was I was too tired to care.

I mark time
in malaria pills
stomach aches and phone calls

They used cats to solve the rat problem on base
so I never saw a rat
just like I only saw the wounded
but never saw the war.

8 years later
and I still smell the chemicals
we used to clean up the blood
in my food and on my hands.

All my friends
say they liked me
better before the war.

The three year old
who lost a hand and a foot
and her eye in the blast
was the lucky one.

The British soldier
went home without arms or legs
like a throw pillow you put on a couch
and forget about.

When I got home
my uncle who served
in Viet Nam said
the real war starts now.

The VA
offers medicine
and therapy
but not answers.

Booze
can't dull the sound
of helicopters or silence.

some days I think I hear helicopters
some days I think I hear bombs
some days I know I hear screams

Beneath a million stars
I used a scalpel
to cut my hand.

Skype would make my 2 year old cry
thinking I was close enough
to come home.

The cigar club
was like a powwow
or prayer circle, looking
for answers in clouds of smoke.

There is a list
of all religious services offered
in a tent no one ever goes in.

The Marine
complained of leg pain
even though everything below his knee
was in a bag down at the burn pit.

My wife
said I liked
you better
when you were gone.

After he left
no matter how hard
we bleached the mattress
it still smelled of pure fear.

The hum of a suction pump
is now the sound
of my sleep.

You can put it in a drawer
with my medals and malaria pills
and all the other stuff I no longer need.

First week back
My wife asks why I just
sit in my chair all day, I tell her
I am waiting for the helicopters.

In 118 degree heat
inside a metal shower stall
I scald myself daily unable to get clean.

The wounded soldier
wanted to talk about being afraid out there
but when I said I haven't been outside the wire
he stopped talking to me all together.

Afghan soldiers
hide western magazines
in their hospital beds to look at
bikini models between prayers.

After awhile
I start to wonder
why we are still surprised
when some body dies.

At first
every wounded Marine
has the face
of my son.

Hannah and my wife
promise each other they will not cry
until after we hang up.

That I cry
at almost everything
finally makes sense.

As he left
a wounded soldier
gave me his winter hat
saying you probably won't need this.

Nurses give pain medication
while corpsmen wrap stumps
and feed the ones without arms.

Their backpacks are lined up
like turtles on a beach
waiting to be put back into the ocean.

The ones who wake up
are usually just happy to be alive
at least for that first day.

Human resources
files the death certificate
while I search through backpacks
for his belongings.

My psychiatrist
can't believe
I still won't take medication.

Who ever thinks
PTSD isn't my wife
and kid's problem
doesn't know them.

The enemy war machine
is made from cell phones
plastic explosives
religion and fear.

I used a tiny scalpel
to carve wooden nails
for the coffin I was afraid
I was taking home.

I never took off
my dog tags in Afghanistan
now I never put them on.

Drinking mouth wash mixed
with cool aid to get a buzz in Afghanistan
is another thing I never thought I would have to do.

Sitting in the waiting room
I don't ask my dad about his cancer
and he doesn't ask me about the war.

About the Author

Matthew Borczon is a nurse and Navy sailor from Erie, Pa. He has published four books of poetry, *A Clock of Human Bones* (Yellow Chair Review), *Battle Lines* (Epic Rites Press), *Capp Road* (Nixes Mate Books), *Ghost Train* (Weasel Publishing), *Sleepless Nights and Ghost Soldiers* (Grey Boarders), and *The Smallest Coffins are the Heaviest* (Epic Rites Punk Chapbook). He was a recipient of the Emerging Artist Grant in his hometown of Erie, Pa. He was nominated for a Pushcart and a Best of the Net for poetry in 2016.

42° 19' 47.9" N   70° 56' 43.9" W

Nixes Mate is a navigational hazard in Boston Harbor used during the colonial period to gibbet and hang pirates and mutineers.

Nixes Mate Books features small-batch artisanal literature, created by writers who use all 26 letters of the alphabet and then some, honing their craft the time-honored way: one line at a time.

nixesmate.pub/books

www.ingramcontent.com/pod-product-compliance
Lightning Source LLC
Chambersburg PA
CBHW052104110526
44591CB00013B/2348